Mummies

King Tut's Tomb:

Ancient Treasures Uncovered

by Michael Burgan

Consultant:

Dr. Salima Ikram

Department of Egyptology

American University in Cairo

Cairo, Egypt

Capstone
press

Mankato, Minnesota

Edge Books are published by Capstone Press,
151 Good Counsel Drive, P.O. Box 669, Mankato, Minnesota 56002.
www.capstonepress.com

Printed in the United States of America in Stevens Point, Wisconsin
082009
005601R

Library of Congress Cataloging-in-Publication Data
Burgan, Michael.
    King Tut's tomb: ancient treasures uncovered / by Michael Burgan.
    p. cm.—(Edge Books, mummies)
    Includes bibliographical references and index.
    ISBN-13: 978-0-7368-3770-5 (hardcover)
    ISBN-10: 0-7368-3770-1 (hardcover)
    ISBN-13: 978-0-7368-6186-1 (softcover)
    ISBN-10: 0-7368-6186-6 (softcover)
    1. Tutankhamen, King of Egypt—Tomb—Juvenile literature.
2. Egypt—Antiquities—Juvenile literature. I. Title. II. Series.
DT87.5.B85 2005
932—dc22   2004010809

Summary: Describes King Tut's tomb, including the treasures found there, King Tut's
mummy, and what scientists have learned from the tomb's discovery.

Editorial Credits
Carrie A. Braulick, editor; Kia Adams, set designer; Jennifer Bergstrom, book designer;
    Kelly Garvin, photo researcher; Scott Thoms, photo editor

Photo Credits
Art Resource, NY/Erich Lessing, cover, 29; Scala, 17, 27; Werner Forman, 16
Corbis/Sandro Vannini, 12; Stapleton Collection, 10; Underwood & Underwood, 4
Getty Images Inc./Time Life Pictures/Mansell, 7, 21, 24
Griffith Institute, Oxford, 15, 18, 20, 23
Mary Evans Picture Library, 22

Table of Contents

Learn About:

- Howard Carter
- The Valley of the Kings
- Discovery of King Tut's tomb

The entrance to King Tut's tomb (front center) is in the Valley of the Kings.

Chapter One

A Discovery in the Valley

Howard Carter was running out of time. The English archaeologist was searching for King Tutankhamen's tomb. King Tutankhamen was an ancient Egyptian king, or pharaoh. Today, he is known as King Tut.

Carter was working in the Valley of the Kings. About 3,000 years ago, the ancient Egyptians buried their pharaohs in this area of southern Egypt.

Some scientists believe King Tut's tomb was built for someone else. It was smaller and had fewer decorations than the tombs of other pharaohs.

Englishman George Herbert, known as Lord Carnarvon, was paying for Carter's search. But Lord Carnarvon was running out of money. He wasn't able to continue paying for Carter's work. Carter knew this search for Tut's tomb would be his last.

Carter had hired workers to dig into the valley's hills. In November 1922, they uncovered a step. After more digging, they found stairs. A wall at the bottom of the stairs blocked an opening into the ground. Carter wondered if his dream of finding King Tut's tomb had come true.

Lord Carnarvon met Carter in Egypt. On November 26, Carter and Carnarvon broke down the wall. They saw a doorway at the end of a tunnel. The doorway was covered in a hard material called plaster.

The Discovery

Carter was eager to find out what was on the other side of the doorway. He cut a small hole in it. Carter then stuck a burning candle in the hole. He peered into the opening.

Carter was amazed by what he saw. Many shiny gold-covered objects filled the room. Later, Carter found other rooms and King Tut's mummy. He spent the next 10 years studying the tomb's treasures.

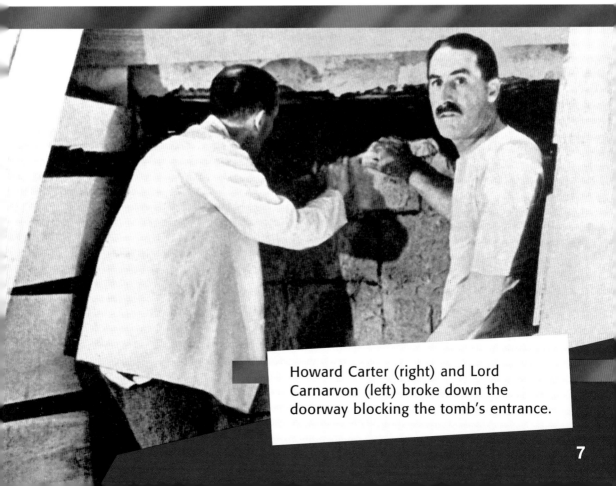

Howard Carter (right) and Lord Carnarvon (left) broke down the doorway blocking the tomb's entrance.

Mediterranean Sea

★ Cairo

EGYPT

Nile River

Red Sea

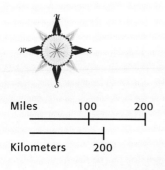

King Tut's Tomb ▲ ● Luxor

| Miles | 100 | 200 |
| Kilometers | 200 | |

Location of King Tut's Tomb

Map Legend

★ Capital City

● City

〰 River

▮ Valley of the Kings

EGYPT

AFRICA

Pharaohs and Their Tombs

The ancient Egyptians believed people had spirits inside their bodies. They thought making dead bodies into mummies would keep the people's spirits alive. The spirits could then live in an afterworld.

Ancient Egyptians thought spirits needed food, clothes, and other supplies in the afterworld. They stored the supplies in mummy tombs. Pharaohs owned huge fortunes. The most valuable objects were stored in their tombs.

King Tut lived in the early 1300s BC. He ruled Egypt for about nine years. King Tut died suddenly at a young age. He didn't have time to build himself a large tomb. But he was still buried with many treasures. Scientists consider King Tut's tomb the most important discovery in the Valley of the Kings. More objects were found in his tomb than in any other ancient Egyptian tomb.

Learn About:
- Rooms of Tut's tomb
- The golden mask
- The sarcophagus

The antechamber held animal-shaped couches and thousands of other objects.

Chapter Two

Inside the Tomb

The riches Carter saw after peeking in Tut's tomb were only the first discoveries. The four rooms in King Tut's tomb held at least 4,000 objects.

The Antechamber

The antechamber was the biggest room in King Tut's tomb. It held several large items. A thin layer of gold covered three couches. These gilded couches were shaped like a cow, a lion, and a figure with body parts from a crocodile and a hippopotamus.

Weapons in Tut's tomb included a dagger.

A wooden throne was under one of the couches. It was covered in gold and decorated with artwork. Lord Carnarvon said it was one of the most amazing pieces of furniture that had ever been found.

Two life-size statues stood by a doorway at one end of the antechamber. The statues acted as guards of the burial chamber. They were supposed to protect King Tut's mummy in the burial chamber.

The Annex

A room called the annex was next to the antechamber. The small size of the annex didn't keep it from holding thousands of objects. They included chests, musical instruments, and jars filled with wine and oil.

Carter found many of King Tut's personal belongings in the annex. King Tut's clothes, games, and weapons were discovered there.

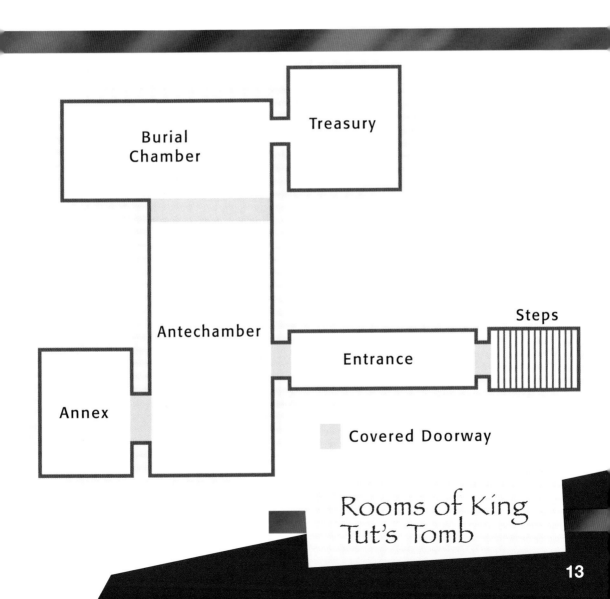

Rooms of King Tut's Tomb

The Burial Chamber

Carter spent several weeks clearing out treasures from Tut's tomb. At last, he was ready to see the king's mummy. He opened the doorway into the burial chamber. Inside, Carter found a large gilded box called a shrine. Three smaller shrines were inside the first one. Artwork decorated the shrines' sides.

Carter found King Tut's sarcophagus inside the last shrine. The lid on this stone coffin was cracked. Carter had a hard time removing the lid.

The Coffins

Carter knew the sarcophagus was not the only thing keeping him from reaching Tut's mummy. He knew the ancient Egyptians placed mummies inside several coffins. Carter found a wooden coffin inside the sarcophagus. A smaller gilded coffin was inside the first one. A third coffin was made of solid gold. It weighed about 240 pounds (110 kilograms). Each coffin had King Tut's face carved into it.

King Tut's mummy was inside the solid gold coffin. A shiny gold mask of Tut's face was on the mummy's head. Fifteen rings decorated the king's fingers.

King Tut's mummy was inside the third coffin.

The Treasury

The burial chamber led to a room called the treasury. The treasury held religious objects. A wooden statue of the ancient Egyptian god Anubis was near the door. Anubis was one of the ancient Egyptians' most important gods. The god was shown as a doglike animal called a jackal.

Tomb Robbers

The ancient Egyptians knew pharaohs' tombs held great riches. Robbers often broke into the tombs. Many of the tombs were almost empty by the time scientists found them. Scientists believe at least two groups of robbers entered Tut's tomb. They think robbers took a gold statue and other valuable objects

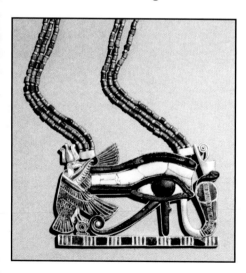

that could be carried easily. If the robbers were caught, they probably suffered a terrible death. The ancient Egyptians punished grave robbers by pushing a large, sharp wooden stick into their bodies.

About 100 small statues of servants called shabti figures were in the room. The statues were meant to do work for the king in the afterworld.

One of the most important objects in the treasury was a large box called a canopic chest. The chest held four jars. An organ from Tut's body was inside each jar. The ancient Egyptians removed the liver, lungs, stomach, and intestines to help preserve the body.

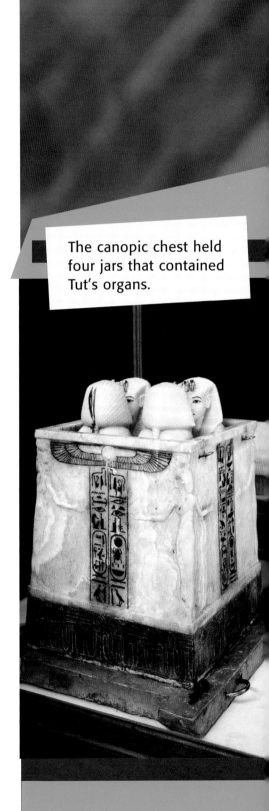

The canopic chest held four jars that contained Tut's organs.

Learn About:

- Damaged wrappings
- The curse of King Tut's tomb
- King Tut's skull

Resin covered the wrappings on King Tut's mummy.

Chapter Three

King Tut's Mummy

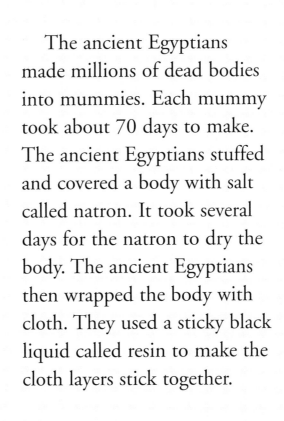

The ancient Egyptians made millions of dead bodies into mummies. Each mummy took about 70 days to make. The ancient Egyptians stuffed and covered a body with salt called natron. It took several days for the natron to dry the body. The ancient Egyptians then wrapped the body with cloth. They used a sticky black liquid called resin to make the cloth layers stick together.

Unwrapping Tut's Mummy

The steps the ancient Egyptians followed to make mummies usually worked well. But something went wrong with King Tut's mummy. In 1925, scientist Douglas Derry cut off the wrappings on Tut's body. He saw black powder. The liquid used to preserve the body had damaged the wrappings and the pharaoh's skin.

Derry studied Tut's mummy. He guessed the king had been about 5 feet, 4 inches (1.6 meters) tall. He thought Tut had been about 18 years old when he died. Derry didn't see signs of injury or disease.

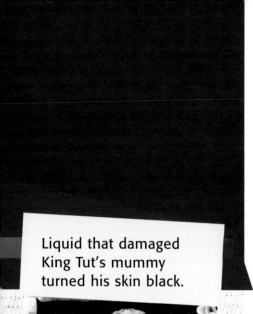

Liquid that damaged King Tut's mummy turned his skin black.

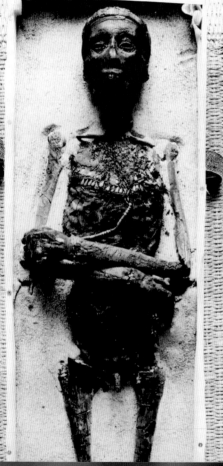

King Tut was not the only person buried in his tomb. Two small coffins held the bodies of baby girls. Scientists believe they may have been King Tut's daughters.

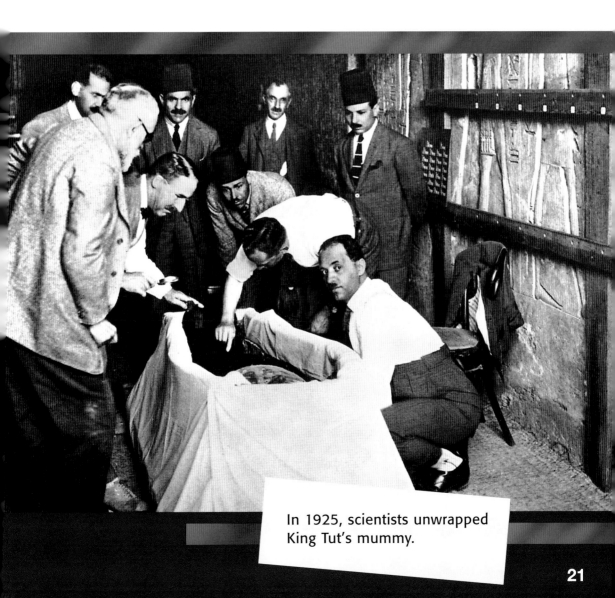

In 1925, scientists unwrapped King Tut's mummy.

The Curse of King Tut's Tomb

In the early 1920s, some people believed that mummy tombs were cursed. They thought people who entered a mummy's tomb would have bad luck. In 1923, newspapers from around the world wrote stories that said King Tut's tomb was cursed. Many people believed the stories.

Lord Carnarvon died about five months after the tomb's discovery. A mosquito bite on his face had become infected. The infection caused him to become sick. People then told more stories about the curse. Some stories said the lights went out in Cairo for five minutes when Lord Carnarvon died. Other stories said Lord Carnarvon's dog in England died at the same time Carnarvon did.

Today, scientists do not believe Lord Carnarvon's death was related to a curse. They believe the idea that mummy tombs can carry curses is just a myth.

Lord Carnarvon

More Studies

In 1968, a group of scientists studied Tut's mummy again. They used an x-ray machine to take pictures of the inside of Tut's body.

The x-rays showed that the bone behind Tut's left ear was thinner than other parts of his skull. The king might have been hit on that spot when he was alive. Some scientists believe the blow was hard enough to kill Tut. This information leads some people to believe that Tut was murdered.

King Tut's skull didn't show signs of injury until it was x-rayed.

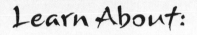

Learn About:

- Ancient Egyptian life
- King Tut's life
- Visiting King Tut's tomb

The many objects found
in King Tut's tomb
made it famous.

Chapter Four

Mysteries Solved

King Tut's tomb is the most famous ancient Egyptian tomb. The many items found there help archaeologists learn more about the ancient Egyptians.

Unlocking Tomb Secrets

Some objects in Tut's tomb helped scientists understand ancient Egyptian daily life. Bread, meat, honey, and other food showed what the ancient Egyptians ate.

Tomb statues and drawings helped scientists learn about religious life.

Some parts of Tut's tomb helped scientists learn about the king. Flowers on King Tut's coffin showed that the king probably died in spring. The gold mask placed over Tut's head revealed what he looked like. A drawing of King Tut hunting may mean he enjoyed the activity. Board games and musical instruments found in the tomb may show other activities of the king.

A Rushed Burial

Scientists noticed that King Tut's tomb was carelessly arranged compared to other pharaohs' tombs. Burial workers seemed to have spent little time preparing it. Few wall decorations were found. The burial shrines were poorly built.

Some people believe Tut's death at a young age left workers with little time to prepare a tomb. Others think the burial was rushed to keep people from learning the cause of his death.

Scientists believe King Tut played a game
called senet on this ivory-topped game board.

Seeing Tut and His Treasures

In the late 1970s, the Egyptian government sent objects from Tut's tomb on world tours. For three years, museums in the United States displayed objects from Tut's tomb. The tours stopped after 1981. Some of the items had been damaged. In 2004, the Egyptian government once again started tours.

Egyptian museums have a large collection of objects from Tut's tomb. The Egyptian Museum in Cairo has the most objects. The Luxor Museum in Luxor also has items from the tomb.

Many tourists go to the Valley of the Kings to explore Tut's tomb. The walls of the burial chamber show Tut and his journey into the afterworld. Tut's sarcophagus sits in the middle of the room. King Tut's mummy rests inside, just as it did after he died more than 3,000 years ago.

Thousands of people visit King Tut's tomb each year.

EDGE FACT

The Luxor Hotel and Casino in Las Vegas, Nevada, has a museum designed to look like King Tut's tomb. Museum visitors can see many re-creations of objects found in the tomb.

Glossary

archaeologist (ar-kee-OL-uh-jist)—a scientist who searches for and studies the items left behind by ancient people to learn about the past

chamber (CHAYM-bur)—a large room

gilded (GIL-ded)—covered with a thin layer of gold

pharaoh (FAIR-oh)—a king of ancient Egypt

plaster (PLASS-tur)—a hard substance made of lime, sand, and water

preserve (pree-ZURV)—to protect something so it stays in its original form

sarcophagus (sar-KAH-fuh-guhs)—a stone coffin; the ancient Egyptians placed inner coffins into a sarcophagus.

spirit (SPIHR-it)—the invisible part of a person that many people believe contains thoughts and feelings; ancient Egyptians believed the spirit left the body after death and traveled to another world.

tomb (TOOM)—a grave, room, or building that holds a dead body

x-ray machine (EKS-ray muh-SHEEN)—a machine that takes pictures of the inside of a body

Read More

Briscoe, Diana. *King Tut: Tales from the Tomb.* Mankato, Minn.: Capstone Press, 2003.

Caselli, Giovanni. *In Search of Tutankhamun: The Discovery of a King's Tomb.* New York: Peter Bedrick Books, 1999.

Kallen, Stuart A. *Mummies.* Wonders of the World. San Diego: Kidhaven Press, 2003.

Internet Sites

FactHound offers a safe, fun way to find Internet sites related to this book. All of the sites on FactHound have been researched by our staff.

Here's how:

1. Visit *www.facthound.com*
2. Type in this special code **0736837701** for age-appropriate sites. Or enter a search word related to this book for a more general search.
3. Click on the **Fetch It** button.

FactHound will fetch the best sites for you!

Index